How Bad Is Your Boss?

SIMON HOLLAND
ILLUSTRATIONS BY
CHUCK GONZALES

To my wife Lindsey and our daughter Rae,
the brand-new Boss of Me.

Text © Simon Holland 2017
Illustrations by Chuck Gonzales
Cover and interior design:
Rosamund Saunders
Cover images © Shutterstock

Skyhorse Publishing books may be
purchased in bulk at special discounts
for sales promotion, corporate gifts,
fund-raising, or educational purposes.

Special editions can also be created to
specifications. For details, contact the
Special Sales Department, Skyhorse
Publishing, 307 West 36th Street, 11th
Floor, New York, NY 10018 or
info@skyhorsepublishing.com.

Visit our website at www.
skyhorsepublishing.com.

10 9 8 7 6 5 4 3 2 1

Library of Congress Cataloging-in-
Publication Data is available on file.

ISBN: 978-1-5107-2129-6

Printed in China

Contents

Introduction:
Rise of the Taskmaster

Given that humans are such self-centered and independent creatures, gifted with a reflective consciousness, a blossoming self-knowledge and a painful awareness of their ultimate insignificance, frailty, and mortality … the concept of having a boss seems somewhat surprising.

More than 12,000 years ago, humans were roaming around the planet as hunter-gatherers, scratching together a living how and where they could. A thousand or so years later, they got a bit more organized and learned how to set up farms. Another thousand years passed, the farms got bigger and turned into settled communities, and some of those communities grew into towns and cities.

All of this was massively hard work. Somewhere along the line, someone had to take control. People needed gainful employment, farms needed staff, cities needed people with crafty skills. When it comes to skills, not everyone has talent—but some people have a real flair for handing out work (otherwise known as delegation) and ordering people around.

Researchers are still trying to find archaeological evidence of the first HR department (in 1992, a rudimentary hole-punch was found in the Levant, but experts are still trying to verify its authenticity), and when they do, we'll know exactly when the first boss was born. But until then, we'll need to draw our own conclusions about the evolution of this universal phenomenon.

"You're not the boss of me" is a battle-cry that emanates from many an office cubicle—the parapets of our modern times—across the length and breadth of the civilized world. But the truth is, we are both shackled and empowered by one very simple transaction: if the boss didn't pay you, you probably wouldn't turn up.

That said, the relationship between the harnessed and the harnesser cuts a lot deeper than this. Like it or not, it's a seminal human relationship. If you're employed by a company, or an individual, chances are you're spending a third of your life in the workplace, which (once you've factored in the commute) is more time than you'll ever spend with your spouse, relatives, friends, or offspring. You also spend at least a third of your life sleeping, to recover from the rigors of work, so you can see how all the important things are being systematically squeezed out of your life by the necessity of having to pay rent.

The boss, therefore, is a figure that looms large in all our lives, and your interactions with him or her are crucial to your future prospects and success. And therein lies the problem: even though the relationship may be flawed, or challenging, it's in your interest to make it work. And let's face it, we are not all leaders. Some of us were born to take orders, while others were destined to take command. It's all part of that rich, vivid tapestry we call the human race—and here, in this humble book, is where we shall begin to unweave it.

EXAMINING YOUR EXECUTIVES

The tests in this book are suggestions of ways in which you can start thinking about your boss from different points of view. Some of the tests are practical, others more observational, but all of them require you to reflect on the methods of your manager and the effects they have on you and your current team of coworkers.

Maybe you think you know your top dog pretty well, having worked with him or her for several years or more. But think again. Once you've started dipping into these tests, you'll hopefully see that there are many subtle layers to the managerial process. The psychological profile of a boss is multi-faceted, and there's a whole host of intricate, interpersonal mechanisms involved in running the show.

Before you proceed …

This might sound a bit like a legal disclaimer on behalf of the publishers, but it needs to be said: nobody wants to see you get fired for using this book indiscriminately and irresponsibly in the workplace. So try and be sensible. Everyone loves a joke, but a gag too many could see you chuckling all the way to The Unemployment Office. The trick is to be as subtle as possible while you're recording the habits, strengths, and foibles of your Head Honcho in his or her natural habitat.

Here's a suggestion (and it's only a suggestion): each day, on your journey to the office, choose a single test to focus on over the ensuing eight hours. You can set up your experiments and make your observations during the course of the working day, reflect on them on the way home, and then write up your results at your leisure. After a week or so, you'll have a chapter's worth of test results to enter into your home-made *How Bad Is Your Boss?* database.

SCORING TIP: as most of the tests in this book are observational, it's a good idea to repeat them a few times to get a more accurate overall score. Use a notepad, perhaps, to record the scores as you work your way through each section. A lot of the questions and scenarios require you to pick out a single result, while some have multiple parts (with different scores available in each)—so make sure you keep a running total.

BOSSING IT: THE TEST CATEGORIES

Ready? Okay. It's time to tiptoe into the lion's den and take
a peek at what makes your taskmasters tick. The tests have
been broken down into four main categories, each one
exploring a different slice of the managerial pie.

TESTS OF THE TRUE BOSS
First of all, we need to work out whether your chiefs of staff
were truly born to be bosses. Is it something that speeds
through their bloodstream, like adrenaline, or is it a role that's
patently at odds with their natural inclinations and personality
types?

TAKE ME TO YOUR LEADER
These tests take a look at the ways in which your bosses
make their presence felt and utilize their position as Head of
the Department. Do they empower you to take control of
your own destiny, or keep you compressed beneath a giant
Thumb of Tyranny?

THE HUMAN FACTOR
Are your chief executives actually just a bunch of real people
in disguise? In this section, you can observe and rate the

ability of your boss to apply his or her personality, wit, and compassion to the challenges of leading a team.

MONARCHS AND MARTYRS

Some bosses will place themselves above you and distance themselves from you in times of corporate conflict. Others see themselves as one of the troops, with a responsibility to join the battle when the going gets tough. The tests in this section will help you to work out where your managers stand along this spectrum.

SCORING TIP: look out for the Scoring Notes in each chapter, which explain how your manager is to be measured. In general, the higher scores reflect a greater level of managerial talent, aptitude, or suitability.

A FINAL NOTE OF CAUTION: try not to let your boss become aware of the testing and observation. He/she probably won't take kindly to it. During your clandestine interactions with the Big Cheese, try to mask your analytical eyes with an expression of "keen interest," "relaxed thoughtfulness," or "measured optimism."

Chapter One

Tests of the True Boss

Some bosses are born leaders. Some of them become great leaders. Others have leadership thrust upon them. So, as you appraise your managers, please do remember that they may not have chosen to be in charge.

That said, it's important to know just how much of a True Boss you have—early on in these proceedings—so that you can make informed judgments about his or her general nature and/or behavior through each of the tests. This chapter will get you nicely warmed up, so that you can get some early points on the board for your current Head Honcho(s).

CHAPTER QUOTIENT: T*B*D POINTS

The scores in this chapter will indicate high, moderate, and lower levels of TBD, or "True Boss DNA."

SCORING NOTE: please remember that "being a boss" is not simply a measure of how thick-skinned and dictatorial a person is. In general, the higher scores indicate a higher level of professionalism and managerial suitability (not a higher level of tyranny and terrible-ness).

1 DELIVERING TRIBUTES

Bosses come in many shapes, sizes, colors, and styles. They range from the Hardline Taskmaster to the Grrreat-guy-who-just-wants-to-be-my-friend. But there's one thing that draws all bosses together into a unified commonality, and it is this: the sublime confidence of being in charge.

One way to test for this awareness is to subtly show your acknowledgment of your superior's supreme leadership. This first experiment will show you how.

Arrive at work early and place a "token of appreciation" on your boss's desk—a humble offering of something that you know he or she really likes, such as a pastry, a piece of fruit, or a book that he or she has been wanting to borrow. Then watch out for the reaction as your beloved Big Cheese discovers the item.

☐ NO REACTION: the item is swept aside or into the inbox in the boss's haste to get to those emails. **NIL POINTS**

☐ NUCLEAR REACTION: the test subject simply glows from his/her inner core (like a radioactive material) in the realization of what the gift signifies. The smile is wide and the eyes sparkle: "I am the boss. I am adored. And I earn the most." **2 POINTS**

☐ CHAIN REACTION: the item not only brings joy, it also initiates something of a carnival atmosphere. Your leader displays the offering prominently and/or parades it around the cubicles. **3 POINTS**

☐ DELAYED REACTION: your boss is so keen to engage with real work that the item is not discovered until mid-morning, when it is greeted with a modest grin.
4 POINTS

☐ CONTROLLED REACTION: the Big Cheese is clearly touched by the gift and instantly, instinctively, knows who has paid the tribute. He or she comes to your desk to thank you, sincerely, humbly, and with no further fanfare.
5 POINTS

2 WEEKEND WORK / BEYOND THE CONTRACTUAL HOURS

It may be that your Head Honcho HATES his or her family, fabricating frequent strategies to avoid spending time with them. Clocking into the office on weekends—or firing up the laptop in some secret, secluded bunker somewhere in the house—is a nifty way of doing this ... but it also means that your own work cell or laptop may go "PING, PING,

PING!!" with incoming emails on a normally sacrosanct
Saturday or Sunday.

**To what extent does your boss expect you to mirror and
match his or her extra-curricular conscientiousness?**

☐ My boss frequently gives me "weekend work" to do, and
schedules a Sunday afternoon call to discuss my progress.
NIL POINTS

☐ Emails escalate to texts (on my PERSONAL cell phone)
if I haven't responded to a work issue on the weekend.
NIL POINTS

☐ My boss barely works during the week, let alone on
weekends. **I POINT**

☐ We've all had the pep talk about "working in a global
industry in which we're expected to be available, even if
that means during off hours, blah blah blaaaaaaaah …"
2 POINTS

☐ My team leader always lets us know if he/she's worked
over the weekend, but only to make us feel guilty and in his/
her debt. **2 POINTS**

☐ I sometimes receive emails on the weekend, but the messages make it clear that no response is expected until Monday (at the earliest). **4 POINTS**

☐ My employer actively discourages working outside our contractual hours. **5 POINTS**

3 PUNCHING THE CLOCK

Many people still refer to checking in and out of work as "punching the clock." It's a bygone phrase that seems ironic, because the average worker's instinct, when the early-morning alarm goes off, is to WHACK that timepiece into oblivion. Like it or loathe it, punctuality is a big deal to some office managers. But just HOW important does your chief timekeeper consider it to be?

Remember: watching the clock isn't necessarily a sign of positive leadership. The agreement you come to, vis-à-vis tolerable levels of tardiness, often depends on a range of mitigating circumstances … A good boss sets the boundaries without binding you up in ridiculous or unrealistic red tape.

I arrived at work ten minutes late today. I apologized. This is what my manager said in reply:

☐ "………….." [Boss had not yet arrived.]
NIL POINTS

☐ "Don't bother taking your coat off. Clear your desk. You're fired." **NIL POINTS**

☐ "Every second that you are late gets added to a spreadsheet I keep on my desktop." **I POINT**

☐ "Don't worry about it. You can work those extra ten minutes at the end of the day." **2 POINTS**

☐ "Ten minutes is not a serious issue!" **3 POINTS**

☐ "Hey, don't worry about it. Delays happen. Looks like you had a terrible journey. Want some coffee? My treat …" **4 POINTS**

☐ "Don't apologize. You've put in some late hours lately. Don't think I haven't noticed. Have we discussed your taking some time off?" **5 POINTS**

4 CORPORATE DOUBLESPEAK

Many of the buzzwords and phrases spoken around the workplace would have George Orwell (creator of the concept of deliberately obscure "Doublespeak" in his dystopian novel, *1984*) scratching his head. So …

It's time to play BOSS BINGO! How many times a day (or week) does your executive supervisor resort to these confusing and often meaningless utterances? On a sheet of paper, make a grid of nine squares (three rows of three) and add the following snippets of regular office jargon—one in each box:

GOING FORWARD …	INCENTIVIZE	IDEA SHOWER
LET'S OWN THE PROBLEM, PEOPLE	LOW-HANGING FRUIT	360-DEGREE THINKING
NOT ENOUGH BANDWIDTH	PARADIGM SHIFT	CORE COMPETENCY

NOTE: feel free to replace any of the above with words or phrases that best suit your work environment.

Once you've composed a Bingo Grid you're happy with, sneak it into a meeting or review. If your boss utters one of the words or phrases, put a cross through that box. At the end of the working week (or five equivalent working days), score the results as follows:

☐ 0–2 boxes crossed off: GENERALLY A "NO BULLSH*T" APPROACH **5 POINTS**

☐ 3–4 boxes crossed off: JUST THE RIGHT SIDE OF THE LINE **4 POINTS**

☐ 5–6 boxes crossed off: HAS READ A BOOK ON MANAGEMENT SPEAK **3 POINTS**

☐ 7–8 boxes crossed off: CAPTAIN CORPORATE **2 POINTS**

☐ ALL boxes crossed off: WOAH, WAY TOO MUCH JARGON!! **1 POINT**

5 WORKSPEAK DECODER

AMBIGUITY BONUS SECTION!

Does your Numero Uno use corporate phraseology to obscure the true meaning of what he or she is saying?

Imagine that your own boss is saying the phrases below and on the next page. Then choose the "translation option" that best expresses what you think your boss is really saying.

"C'MON PEOPLE …"

"LET'S SPITBALL SOME IDEAS."

☐ Translation option one: "I genuinely would like your input."
3 POINTS

☐ Translation option two: "I've been given a difficult task, which I want you all to complete on my behalf."
2 POINTS

☐ Translation option three: "I didn't prepare anything for this meeting." **1 POINT**

"LET'S THINK OUTSIDE THE BOX ON THIS ONE."

☐ Translation option one: "I don't want the same old crap you guys came up with last time." **1 POINT**

☐ Translation option two: "I'm looking for some original thinking, and I know that you guys can deliver."
3 POINTS

☐ Translation option three: "If we can write enough zany ideas down, it'll take longer for the senior execs to realize how average they all are." **I POINT**

"LET'S REACH OUT TO OUR GLOBAL COWORKERS TO GET THIS SOLVED."

☐ Translation option one: "I don't want to waste my department's time with this dumb-ass assignment."
2 POINTS

☐ Translation option two: "If you can't think of any ideas, steal someone else's (and make sure we get the credit for it)."
I POINT

☐ Translation option three: "Company-wide collaboration always pays dividends, and it also takes some of the pressure off my team." **3 POINTS**

TOTAL SCORE: ____

6 W*E*P*S*A: WORK EMAIL PORTAL SEPARATION ANXIETY

Does your manager prize his or her phone so much that a knitted pouch has been created for it? Or has he or she purchased a bling case on eBay?

If so, here's an enjoyable (albeit highly immature) activity that ought to be a bit of a blast: so long as you know your boss well enough (and are certain that he or she won't spontaneously combust through stress). Try hiding his or her phone in the office (somewhere safe, i.e., not in the tropical fish tank) and then monitor the response when he or she fails to locate it.

Oh. What. Fun.

Upon discovering that his/her work cell was not on the desk, where he/she left it …

☐ LOSS OF TEMPER: a primal, gut-churning cry jolted everyone from their work, "WHO MOVED MY GOD-DAMNED PHONE?!!" **NIL POINTS**

☐ LOSS OF REVENUE: everyone was asked to stop work and join the search (with an estimate of $82,000 in lost earnings). **NIL POINTS**

☐ LOSS OF PERSPECTIVE: the face went white, the body slumped into the chair, the head fell to the chest, and henceforth was heard the unmistakable sound of gentle weeping. **1 POINT**

☐ LOSS OF DIGNITY: that dusty suit is a tell-tale sign of somebody who has just spent an hour crawling around the office floor. **1 POINT**

☐ CAPTAL IDEA: my boss shrugged, grabbed his/her personal phone, and waltzed out for lunch. **3 POINTS**

☐ CAPITAL GAINS: my boss made a quick call to IT, asking for an immediate replacement. **4 POINTS**

7 ANNUAL LEAVE

Getting time off work is never as easy as it ought to be, huh? Vacation arrangements can be hard to lock down, there's never a good time to put your work on hold, clients and colleagues pile on the pressure when they know you're going away, and you have to work twice as hard (or twice the hours) before and after the break to keep your professional life on track … and then, in addition to all that, you have to square up to the Big Kahuna and ask him or her to authorize the annual leave.

Generally speaking, whenever I request some time off, my manager turns into (please choose ONE of the following) …

☐ DELIBERATOR: he'll/she'll "think about it" and get back to me (at some vague and unspecified point in the future).
NIL POINTS

☐ EMOTIONAL MANIPULATOR: he/she reminds me that he/she hasn't had any time off "all year," and then slowly … hesitantly … reluctantly signs my request form.
1 POINT

☐ INQUISITOR: he/she flips a lamp so it is shining in my direction and hits me with questions: "Where are you going?"; "What'll you be doing?"; "How much does a vacation like that cost these days?" **2 POINTS**

☐ ADMINISTRATOR: he/she systematically checks my remaining vacation allowance and then (as long as I have enough days left) authorizes the time off immediately.
3 POINTS

☐ FEEL-GOOD FACILITATOR: he/she stands up, embraces me, and says, "You deserve it. You've earned it. You OWN it. Have a great time." **4 POINTS**

8 TEA TOTALITARIANISM

Preparing a hot beverage for the Big Chief (especially if it's a brand-new employer) can be a daunting experience. How do they take it? Will they reject it if it's not up to par? Will it affect your bonus or promotion prospects if you stir in too many sugars? Will you be referred to HR if the cappuccino has the wrong ratio of espresso to foam?

When it comes to making tea and coffee, my boss is …

☐ ANALLY RETENTIVE: he/she insists that I keep the tea bag in the cup for a SPECIFIC amount of time, to brew, before a clearly defined measure of milk is added.

I POINT

☐ OVERLY DESCRIPTIVE: as part of my induction training, he/she supervised my first visit to the staff kitchen and walked me through the finer points of the cappuccino machine. **2 POINTS**

☐ COLOR-CODED: this guy has a color chart on the office wall, to help us make coffees for all the execs.

2 POINTS

☐ NOT FUSSED: this taskmaster takes it as it comes. All that matters is the regular caffeine hit. **4 POINTS**

☐ FAIR-MINDED: my Numero Uno does his/her fair share of the coffee rounds, and probably makes more drinks for the team than vice versa. **5 POINTS**

Chapter Two

TAKE ME TO YOUR LEADER

If a bunch of inquisitive (and hopefully mild-mannered) alien colonists strolled into your office—having collected their visitor passes from the Front Desk, obviously—and took a good look at every single member of your team as they stood around the watercooler … would they be able to tell the Queen Bee from the Drones, the Kingpin from the humble Retainers?

What sort of aura of leadership and control do your Number One Execs exude from their inner nuclei of power? Is it there for all to see, or do your Foremost Forepeople hide their leading lights under a businesslike bushel? Are you basking in the supportive glow of a Superior Supervisor, or begging for scraps of acknowledgment from a much more Enigmatic Executive?

Double Gee whiz, if your leaders don't present themselves well, maybe those aliens will end up taking control!

CHAPTER QUOTIENT: G*G or "Double Gee" POINTS

The scores in this chapter will indicate superior, medium, or inferior GG, or "Guru Grades."

SCORING NOTE: these scores are not necessarily a measure of likeability or coolness. A manager may choose to be stand-offish and emotionally lukewarm, but he or she may also have your best interests at heart. And don't be seduced by a Charismatic Controller who claims to have you in line for promotion. This person could be playing a game all of his or her own (with you and your teammates as the pawns).

1 THE CHARISMA QUOTIENT

Picture the scenario: it's been a good month, revenue's up, and a staff social event has been announced. Keynote speakers have been appointed. A room at the local bar has been reserved. Excitement is in the air. Potato chips are in bowls. At least one free drink is guaranteed. There are rumors of pretzels; everyone shows up.

But the question is: how do your bosses behave at events such as these? How do they work the room? Do they wear their status on their sleeves, pulling rank, or step back and let the junior staff members express themselves (within reasonable boundaries of professionalism and good taste)?

Take a look at the "Principal Padrone" profiles on the following pages. See if you can match your "superior" to one of the descriptions. If so, your boss could earn some interesting Double Gees.

☐ THE SLEAZE: forget perfume or aftershave—coat yourself in repellant. **NIL POINTS**

☐ THE LOOSE CANNON: saucy suggestions and dangerous indiscretions abound in this executive's orbit. The personal lives of the board members have never had so much airtime. **I POINT**

the Sleaze

The Loose Cannon

☐ THE SHOWMAN/WOMAN: truly makes his/her presence felt, leaving nobody in any doubt as to who put the money behind the bar. **1 POINT**

☐ THE SHAMAN: a crowd has gathered around this seemingly "sacred" shaman. Either he's/she's spiked their drinks, or he/she has some other preternatural hold over them (e.g., information about the bonus situation).
2 POINTS

The show man

The Shaman

☐ THE MAVERICK: if you really want to know how this company ought to be run, buy this person a drink and give an ear to what he/she has to say. **2 POINTS**

☐ THE ENIGMA: this is a lean-to-the-wall, back-of-the-room boss, happy to listen, wait, and watch while giving nothing of him/herself away. **3 POINTS**

the Maverick

The Enigma

☐ THE PHILOSOPHER: you end up glued to this person's thoughts and feelings about issues that go waaaaay beyond the office walls. Wow, he's/she's more than just a pencil-pusher. **4 POINTS**

☐ THE COMMON MAN/WOMAN: relieved to be free of the hierarchy for a night, this person wants to blend in and find out all about YOU, while also being careful not to overstep the mark. **5 POINTS**

The Philosopher

The Common woman/man

2 MICRO- AND MACRO-MANAGEMENT

At last, we come to the business of "the job" itself. Managing the workload of a whole department is something of an art. We know that the top hunter-gatherers of the Mesolithic period had it figured out, because how else would you topple a woolly mammoth? The ancient Sumerians and Egyptians had a good hold over their human resources, too. The Romans had a great management structure—everyone knew where they stood and what their job description was. Like them or loathe them, the 13th-century Mongols were equally well-organized. Genghis Khan was a ruthless leader, but he united his team (and kept all their employee reviews neatly on file).

So—in the global, corporate world of the 21st century, our managers should be highly evolved leaders who always get the balance right ... Right?

How intensively does your chief of staff keep tabs on your day-to-day tasks?

☐ NO HANDS: my boss very rarely knows what I'm doing and how I'm doing it. I'd be grateful for some guidance now and again. **NIL POINTS**

☐ HEAVY-HANDED: my boss checks pretty much every detail of my work. I don't feel as if he/she trusts me to get it right on my own. **NIL POINTS**

☐ HANDS-OFF: my boss is so hands-off that I sometimes think there's no one at the wheel of this ship. **I POINT**

☐ HANDS-ON: my boss is well aware of my workload, but sometimes so hands-on that I can barely get my own fingers on the keyboard. **2 POINTS**

☐ HANDS UP, PLEASE: my boss has a laissez-faire style but trusts us to get on with things and let him/her know when support is required. **3 POINTS**

☐ EVEN-HANDED: my boss is happy for me to take on some managerial stuff occasionally, but only when I can handle the extra workload. **4 POINTS**

☐ HELPING HANDS: my boss knows my strengths and weaknesses. He/she nurtures where it's needed, empowers when appropriate. **5 POINTS**

3 MR. OR MRS. MOTIVATOR

Whether you're motivated, de-motivated, or indifferently motivated at work usually depends on a range of factors, such as the workload, your enthusiasm for the work, the work environment, your relationship with your coworkers, and your longer-term prospects at the company. You may also have some personal stuff going on, now and again, which can toss an extra curveball of unhappiness into the mix.

If the morale of an individual (or the team as a whole) takes a dive, it's up to your leaders to pull on their Guru Gloves and handle the problem. They may even be the cause of the issue, which means they'll need to be self-reflective and flexible enough to listen to your feedback and make a few changes. Somehow, they need to restore your faith and your energy ... Hey, that's why they get paid the big bucks!

How does your boss pick you up when you're down?

☐ It's hard to keep your mojo when you know how much your boss despises his/her job. **NIL POINTS**

☐ When I complained about my workload, my manager sent me away to a How To Manage Your Workload workshop. **1 POINT**

☐ My boss means well, but his/her pep talks tend to backfire. We always leave the staff meeting less motivated than when we went in. **2 POINTS**

☐ I lost out on promotion. My boss made some time for me, took me for coffee, and made it clear that my next opportunity was not far away. **3 POINTS**

☐ My boss is irrepressibly positive, a naturally enthusiastic, optimistic, and upbeat person. The good vibes rub off on everybody in the team. **4 POINTS**

☐ My supervisor seems to be some kind of psychic. He's/she's totally tuned into those times when we're over-stretched, or when morale is low, and takes time out to help us find a solution. **5 POINTS**

4 HOLDING THE FORT

Remember the Alamo? Back in 1836, the manager of a fortress in San Antonio, Texas, popped out for a pint of milk for the staff kitchen (because that 13-day siege had left the cupboards bare). He was only gone for about ten minutes, but when he got back he found that 1,500 Mexicans had marched in and eaten all the cookies.

Needless to say, heads rolled. That kind of delegation debacle can damage a boss's confidence in his deputies. It's a two-way street: you need to prove that you can handle the office when the taskmaster's outta town, and he or she needs to trust you with the keys to the filing cabinet (where else would you hide the cookies?).

Does your chief ever put you in charge?

☐ Are you kidding? My boss doesn't trust me with a stapler, let alone the wifi password. **NIL POINTS**

☐ My supervisor's always happy for me to take responsibility for the running of the department, so that he/she doesn't have to. **I POINT**

☐ If I'm needed to take charge of the office, even for just a day, my boss calls in every hour to check I haven't bankrupted us or burned the place down. **2 POINTS**

☐ I frequently chair meetings on behalf of my boss, when he's/she's out of the office or taking an important call. **3 POINTS**

☐ When my manager goes on vacation, he/she leaves lots of helpful notes, so that I have everything I need in case I have to stand in for him/her. **4 POINTS**

☐ In my appraisal, my senior exec made it clear that he/she wanted me to step up and take the lead on a few things, to give me a bit of managerial experience. **5 POINTS**

5 PASSING IT DOWN (A.K.A. THE POOP CHUTE)

Delegation. It can be a divisive concept. In the right hands, it's a tool of great leadership and the scaffolding of a well-managed department. In the wrong hands, it's a weapon of mass destruction.

Our chiefs of staff have the freedom to manage "upwards," "downwards," "sideways"—and even "slantways"—but do they always do it effectively? How, when, and why a manager delegates is a huge indicator as to how suitable he/she is to lead.

What sort of passer-downer is your supervisor?

☐ MIDDLING MANAGER: anything delegated to my boss, by the senior execs, simply gets typed into an email and passed on to me. There's no filter. **NIL POINTS**

☐ POOP SHOOTER: he/she only delegates the crap and the menial scraps, none of the interesting stuff. **I POINT**

☐ FLOW STOPPER: he's/she's too much of a control-freak. The staff members are bored, while he's/she's stressed and overworked. **2 POINTS**

☐ CHORE CHECKER: My boss always checks on my workload before delegating down. **3 POINTS**

☐ FLOW REVERSER: I am encouraged to delegate upwards to my boss, should my workload get too taxing. **4 POINTS**

☐ EMPOWERER: My manager prefers to delegate the tasks that will help me to develop my responsibilities and build my career. **5 POINTS**

6 STAFF RETREAT DESTINATIONS

The Staff Retreat or Team-Building Day is a monolith of our modern times. It stands there, on the corporate calendar, like an immovable obstacle. You can't go around it, you can't tunnel under it, you can't climb over it—although you might be set the task of constructing a bridge (using a specified range of materials) to support the weight of a junior intern named Jill. No ifs, no buts—you've just got to go through with it.

Before we talk about the potential content and atmosphere of the retreat, let's look at a preliminary question: where does your boss normally take you on your team-building adventures?

What's the usual setting for your training and/or team-building days?

☐ COP OUT: the boss took us on a short trip to the fabled Top Floor, the executive area with the fluffy carpet and the "slightly nicer" view of the industrial park. **I POINT**

☐ FUN DAY OUT: in an obvious bid to win our favor, our exec took us to an amusement park. It was fun. I won a stuffed animal toy, but there wasn't much else to report at the de-briefing. **2 POINTS**

☐ MISSING IN ACTION: we all met up in a hotel conference room. We were greeted by a team of professional training facilitators. It was a great day—but the boss was nowhere to be seen. **3 POINTS**

☐ HAVING YOUR SAY: our manager asked us to submit ideas of where we'd like to go on our staff retreat. He/she then made all the arrangements. **4 POINTS**

☐ MIXING IT UP: we started the day at an art gallery, completed a fun challenge, then we got taken to lunch, swapping seats with every course so that we could mingle. In the afternoon, we got on with an outdoor training exercise. **5 POINTS**

7 THE TRAINING DAY DYNAMIC

Okay, so you've made it to the conference center, training venue, or some other pile of bricks you've been asked to schlep out to for training. On the way, you've downed enough coffee to keep a team of laborers awake for a week. There's no escaping the fact that you'll be stuck in the same airless room for the entire day, forced to team up and cooperate with people you'd normally do your best to avoid.

The Staff Retreat can engender an awkward, enforced dynamic. Some bosses are masters at planning these events, appointing facilitators that can keep people energized and engaged, mixing things up and changing the pace to keep the clock spinning nicely toward "wine o'clock." Others don't think things through and place way too much pressure on the trainees to power through the activities.

Think back to your last day of training and/or team building. Was it fun, informative, stimulating, or just a bunch of futile hours that you'll never get back?

☐ The physical team-building exercises were cringeworthy, excruciating, and borderline inappropriate. At times, I felt physically violated. **NIL POINTS**

☐ There was a motivational speaker. He'd been poorly briefed. He talked to us for an hour about the importance of Looking After Number One. We all work in the care industry.
1 POINT

☐ It was good to get out of the office for a day, but a lot of the training was irrelevant. I'd have preferred smaller groups doing more skill-based exercises. **2 POINTS**

☐ Our boss knows us well and really understands our sense of humor. The day was a blast, full of fun, games, laughs, and smiles. **3 POINTS**

☐ I'm usually pretty skeptical about training days, but the last one was really well pitched, relevant, and constructive. Gave me loads to think about. **4 POINTS**

8 STAFF TURNOVER

Some leaders inspire great loyalty from their staff. Look at Robert Falcon Scott: he took his team on one of the most challenging Staff Retreats of all time, all the way to the South Pole. And when they got there, they found that their corporate rivals from Norway had out-performed them. The adventure did not end well, but it's a tale of people sticking together through thick and thin to achieve a common goal, no matter how treacherous the terrain.

These days, people quit their jobs for all sorts of reasons. Sometimes the lure of a better salary, title, pay scale, and prospects is just too good to pass up. That said, a good boss can be an asset worth holding on to.

Is your boss a hirer, a firer, an inspirer—or a mixture of these?

☐ CONSTANT REVOLUTIONS: people get hired and fired all the time. We've had to install a revolving door to cope with all the comings and goings. **NIL POINTS**

☐ MARKET AVERAGE: the staff turnover is similar to that of other companies I've worked for. It rises and falls, depending on the state of the jobs market. **1 POINT**

☐ A LACK OF PRUNING: if anything, my boss should be a bit more brutal and cut away some of the dead wood doing little but pulling in their fat salaries. **2 POINTS**

☐ REMARKABLE RETENTION: over the past few years hardly anyone has left. We've got a pretty stable team.
3 POINTS

☐ TALISMANIC: when I talk about how good my manager is, people often say, "Can you give him my résumé?"
4 POINTS

☐ POTENTIAL MUTINY: if ever my boss was fired, I think the whole department might walk out. **5 POINTS**

Chapter Three

THE HUMAN FACTOR

Throughout your clandestine explorations of boss-like behavior, you should try to compile evidence of your employer's reactions to social, interpersonal, and emotive stimuli. Being a boss is like walking a tightrope between kind-hearted approachability, on the one side, and impenetrable stoicism on the other. Between these two extremes lies the chasm into which your leader may fall—and, if you're not careful, he or she might drag you down too! So it's not just about your boss, it's about you as well. How much emotional strain do you place on your employers, and how much compassion are they able to extend to you in return?

In short: are your chief executives actually just a bunch of real people in disguise?

CHAPTER QUOTIENT: H*Q POINTS

The scores in this chapter will indicate a high, medium, or low HQ, or "Human Quotient."

SCORING NOTE: when scoring this section, you need to bear in mind how appropriate it is (given the situation or emotional context) for your boss to react in the various ways described. Your manager is not paid to be your best friend, but there's a middle ground in which they can address the problems or challenges you may be experiencing. What they are paid to do (generally speaking) is facilitate the right support for you in times of difficulty. The scores in this section aim to reflect this tricky balance.

1 INTERPERSONAL SKILLS (TO PAY DA BILLS)

This is a tricky series of tests, depending on the type of environment you work in. Some managers have their hands tied when it comes to reaching out to their employees in need, whereas others would be hung out to dry if their compassion was not immediately forthcoming. Remember: what you're judging is humanness in the workplace.

As with all scientific experiments, it's important to find a control or base level from which to measure your results. So, to get you started, here are a few common settings and scenarios you might encounter in the workplace, which should give you an opportunity to grade your foreperson and calibrate his/her interpersonal instruments.

Please match your Big Kahuna to his/her most likely reaction in each of the five scenarios:

SCENARIO ONE: when a colleague on maternity leave brought in her new baby, my boss …

☐ … shut down his/her computer and left for lunch.
1 POINT

☐ … made it clear that we could all take half an hour off to chat with the new mom. **2 POINTS**

☐ … said it would be best if we all went out for an early lunch, so that we'd have more time to visit. **3 POINTS**

SCENARIO TWO: whenever anyone leaves the department, my boss …

☐ … delegates the leaving arrangements (and speech) to another member of the team. **1 POINT**

☐ … takes responsibility for the goodbye speech, and delivers it him/herself. **2 POINTS**

☐ … encourages us all to contribute ideas to the goodbye speech, so that it's full of personal memories and silly anecdotes. **3 POINTS**

SCENARIO THREE: if a team member suffers a personal problem, my boss …

☐ … normally assumes that a more junior member of the team will address the problem, offer comfort, and then escalate the issue to him/her if necessary. **1 POINT**

☐ … immediately insists that he/she should take some time off or go on personal leave. **2 POINTS**

☐ … spends some time with the employee to discuss the problem, in order to work out how best to support him/her.
3 POINTS

SCENARIO FOUR: when a neighbor called to say my apartment was flooded, my boss said …

☐ "Can your neighbor let a plumber in for you, so you can stay at work?" **NIL POINTS**

☐ "You'd better go home and call a plumber. Can you work from home until it's all fixed?" **I POINT**

☐ "Here's the number of a great plumber. We'll look after your work until it's safe for you to come back."
3 POINTS

SCENARIO FIVE: whenever I call in sick, my boss …

☐ … always seems slightly skeptical on the phone.
NIL POINTS

☐ … asks about my symptoms and offers advice.
I POINT

☐ … insists I take enough time off for recovery, rather than rushing back before I'm better. **3 POINTS**

TOTAL HQ SCORE: _____

2 BROAD SHOULDERS

Bosses blessed with a hard shell will take anything that the office environment can throw at them, from an aggressively jammed photocopier to a full-scale office walkout. Such shoulders of stone will be able to withstand the strain, but are they permeable enough to absorb the blood, sweat, and tears of a junior colleague who's just put in an 18-hour shift?

Just how moist are your supervisor's shoulders?* Have they been cried on a few times, or are they strangers to that kind of emotional precipitation?

*[If this book had been written in the 1980s, a quick squeeze of a female VP's shoulder pads would've given you a clue. These days, you'll need to work a bit harder to make your observations. Read on …]

So—just how emotionally resilient is your Numero Uno?

☐ THE TICKING BOMB: shows up stinking of cigarettes (and sometimes booze); freaks out on a daily basis, often turning the air blue with a fireworks display of expletives.
NIL POINTS

☐ WARNING SIGNALS: displays tacit visual indications of stress (e.g., red eyes, hunched shoulders), but only occasionally vents the tension verbally. **1 POINT**

☐ THE MARTYR: constantly busy, absorbing all the pressure exerted on the department, but rarely manages to engage with staff on a one-to-one basis. **2 POINTS**

☐ THE ADRENALINE JUNKIE: unflappable and fast-paced. Thrives under the pressure like an extreme sports enthusiast.
3 POINTS

☐ THE PEOPLE MANAGER: clearly a workaholic, but always makes time to person-manage the staff and their workloads. **4 POINTS**

☐ THE HUMAN DAM: silently pushes back on the waterfall of demands cascading down from senior management, in order to control and protect the workloads of the whole team. **5 POINTS**

3 THE TRUST TRANSACTION

Your relationship with your professional superiors is like a wind-up clock that you need to keep in good condition, well oiled and steadily ticking. Don't let it slow and stagnate—but don't overwind it, either. If the pendulum starts to swing too wildly, you might end up with an employee–employer interaction that strays far too far into the realms of familiarity.

The name of the game can be summed up in a single word: trust. Don't wax lyrical at work about your inner thoughts, opinions, feelings—and personal entanglements—until you feel you can depend on the discretion of your Top Dog. The hour hands on that clock may need to spin around many times before that level of faith is established.

How much confidence do you feel you can invest in your Head Honcho?

☐ My boss knows what's on my résumé, but very little else about the real me. **NIL POINTS**

☐ I only get as far as small talk with my manager.
I POINT

☐ He/she likes to get us out for drinks so that we'll spill the beans about our personal lives. **2 POINTS**

☐ I'd say we're professional colleagues when we're in the office, and we're as relaxed and open as friends when we're not at work. **3 POINTS**

☐ He's/she's been a good support during some tough times—understanding but non-intrusive. **4 POINTS**

☐ My boss is interested in my life outside the office, and supportive of my personal commitments, but never pumps me for intimate information. **5 POINTS**

4 SOCIAL MEDIA MANAGEMENT

One of the most awkward situations known to humankind
(apart from turning up to work in the same outfit as
someone else) is receiving a social media contact request
from a member of the senior management team. Should
you ignore the invitation or accept it on diplomatic
grounds? In either case, you're damned if you do and you're
damned if you don't.

Striking up such an online connection is like strapping a TV
camera to your head (and/or other bodily appendages) and
opening up the lead-lined doors that separate your working
life from the private, velvet-upholstered boudoirs of your
deeper, more enigmatic self. So if you don't want unsolicited
eyes peeping in and logging on, keep those virtual doors
locked and bolted.

How would you describe your supervisor's attitude toward or use of social networking sites?

☐ CREEPY INQUISITOR: when I come into work Monday morning, my boss sometimes quizzes me about stuff posted on my Facebook profile over the weekend. **NIL POINTS**

☐ SPACE INVADER: I sometimes feel as if my boss is trying to access my personal life, or connect with my friends, via social media. **NIL POINTS**

☐ OVERSHARER: my boss reveals way too much about him/herself on social networking sites. Hard to ignore, even harder to stomach. **NIL POINTS**

☐ PRIVATE DANCER: my boss has no time for social networking sites—and if he/she does have a profile, I've seen nothing of it. **2 POINTS**

☐ POLICY PRO: my boss does not permit social media access during core work hours; no work-related material, issues, or conversations are to be shared on networking sites.
3 POINTS

☐ SAFE SURFER: my boss and I have connected on professional networking sites, such as LinkedIn, but not on social media sites. **4 POINTS**

5 WATER-COOLER CASUALITY

Managers or team leaders often fall into one of two categories: those who genuinely want you to like them and those who absolutely could not care less if you added their profile picture to the office dartboard. There are, however, those that fall somewhere in between.

Ever visited the kitchen or water cooler to exchange a bit of clandestine gossip with a coworker? If so, try and time your next visit so that it is within earshot or viewing distance of your boss and/or coincides with his or her walk past on the way back from a meeting. Make a note of any ensuing reactions to your secretive summit.

How does your boss react to this intimate moment
between two colleagues?

☐ DIRECT LINE: the manager comes straight over and butts
in on the conversation. **1 POINT**

☐ BUGGED OUT: your boss will be able to re-play your
conversations later, as he or she has installed a surveillance
device (check the nearby potted plants). **1 POINT**

☐ IPHONE PHONEY: the test subject hovers nearby,
pretending to make or take a personal phone call, in order to
overhear the juicy goss. **2 POINTS**

☐ PARANOID ANDROID: the subject instantly believes
that he or she is the subject of the chatter. The boss fakes a
trip to the cooler to find out. **2 POINTS**

☐ STRICTEST CONFIDENCE: the taskmaster comes over
and demands that you return to your desks. You have to
admire the directness of the tactic. **2 POINTS**

☐ TOO COOL FOR THE COOLER: such idle chatter does not bother the boss. He or she simply leaves you to it.

4 POINTS

☐ KNOWING BUT NICE: the guy in charge smiles or nods, letting you know that he/she is okay with a bit of time out shared between colleagues—but that you're encouraged to resume work shortly. **5 POINTS**

6 APPRAISE ME (LIKE YOU SHOULD)

To be honest, we could dedicate an entire chapter (or book) to the core language and dynamics of The Staff Review, but sadly there's not enough time and space in the universe to cover each of its subtle aspects in detail. So let's just round up a few of the fundamentals—the time, setting, and atmosphere that your manager has facilitated (either consciously or unconsciously) in order to set you at ease (or do the exact opposite?) through the course of your six-month reviews.

Has he or she devised an exercise that aims to put you and your future prospects under the spotlight, or designed a more ego-driven campaign to remind you that your career is subject to the whims of a Higher Power? Also, look out for the personal and/or creative touches that your Big Cheese may have put in place to reveal—often very subtly—their true opinion of you, the appraisee.

At the very beginning of my appraisal …

☐ I was handed my pink slip. **NIL POINTS**

☐ A large, windowless van pulled up outside the office. A guy got out and told me to "Hop in the back." I was blindfolded and taken to an industrial park on the edge of town. Eventually, I heard my boss's voice asking me, "Where do you see yourself in five years' time?" **I POINT**

☐ I went down to the staff cafeteria as my boss forgot to book a private room for my review. My boss turned up half an hour later. **I POINT**

☐ My boss handed me two tickets to a Broadway show and said, "Why don't we loosen up a bit before we do this thing?" **2 POINTS**

☐ A cup of coffee (made the way I like it) and a plate of my favorite cookies were waiting for me in the meeting room. **3 POINTS**

☐ Right off the bat, my manager said, "I think we need to do something about your salary, don't we?" **4 POINTS**

☐ My team leader said I could choose the place and time for the appraisal, and was keen for me to set the agenda for the first half of the meeting. **5 POINTS**

7 OFFICE PARTY B*L*D (BODY LANGUAGE DECODER)

It's that time of year again: the annual office shindig is looming large, an event as much feared as it is eagerly anticipated. Before you leave for the party venue, check your jacket pockets and/or purse for the following essentials: cash and cards (for when the free bar runs dry); chewing gum and/or breath-freshening mints; emergency banana (for lining the stomach prior to tequila shots); deodorant (for the latter stages of the evening); contraceptives (you never know); keys to your house/apartment; cell number of a trusted friend; a spare pair of underpants (you never know); map of the city (in case you fall asleep on the last bus/train/subway service).

But, hang on a minute! You've forgotten the one thing you should never enter the party without—your corporate BLD (Body Language Decoder). How else are you going to interpret the silent communications of the senior management figures attending this star-spangled event? Take heed of this two-part test, take note—and take care.

PART ONE: MANAGERIAL MINGLING

Watch out for the following party postures and score your boss accordingly:

☐ THE CLOSED DOOR: hands thrust into pockets, gaze directed at the floor, this boss is not open to the business of casual conversation. **NIL POINTS**

☐ GAME OF THRONES: a 100% seated stance that requires lesser mortals to visit and bestow their meek attentions upon the senior executive. **I POINT**

☐ ANTI-SOCIAL SURVEY: this point-to-point surveillance technique allows the supervisor to remain in the shadows, tuning into scraps of conversation until he/she has figured out whether there's anyone worth talking to. **I POINT**

☐ CATCH'YER IN THE EYE: a sly stalker who'll shuffle around for as long as it takes to lock you into eye contact, engage the conversational tractor beam, and then you're DOOOOOMED!! **2 POINTS**

☐ ROOM SWEEPER: an open, striding, confident stance that says, "I'm not just your boss, I'm a raconteur—stop me as I make my rounds if you want a batch of my witty wisecracks."

3 POINTS

☐ THE OPEN BOOK: arms loose and relaxed, feet planted shoulder-width apart, this stance says, "Like a notebook with a broken spine, I am approachable and open to ideas."

5 POINTS

PART TWO: ON THE DANCE FLOOR

As the evening progresses, check to see how your boss is expressing him/herself on the dance floor:

☐ GROPE AND GRIND: a sequence of desperate attempts at inappropriate bodily contact. **NIL POINTS**

☐ TEENAGE MAN CLUB: the floor becomes a sweaty mosh pit of his/her own creation. **1 POINT**

☐ FLIRTY MOMMA: silky and seductive moves, occasionally crossing the line into smoldering eye contact.
2 POINTS

☐ DAD'S CLUB 7: those middle-aged execs who are only too happy to embarrass themselves. More endearing than annoying. **3 POINTS**

☐ WALLFLOWER: a cheerful sideline spectator, dignity intact. **4 POINTS**

☐ LO-FI BOPPER: subtle, simple sways and bobs; the right kind of self-consciousness. **5 POINTS**

8 SECRET SANTA E*G*D (ESSENTIAL GIFT DECODER)

While we're on the subject of end-of-year parties, we really ought to examine the hidden language—or cryptology, if you will—of the Secret Santa gift.

In case you are unfamiliar with this concept, let's explain: the name of each staff member is scrawled on a piece of paper and put into a hat (for example). Each person picks out a name at random—this is the coworker for whom they'll buy a present, keeping to an agreed upon price range (for example, between $5 and $10.) Purchasing the present is an interesting experience, but the fun really begins at the party, when staff unwrap gifts publicly and guess who purchased them.

Let's imagine your BOSS has picked out your name from the Secret Santa pool. Here are some general categories of items that he/she might buy, along with the potential meaning of each gift:

☐ AN EXECUTIVE STRESS DOLL = "You need to chill out, you do my head in." **NIL POINTS**

☐ MINIATURE BOTTLES OF LIQUOR = "Easy option."
1 POINT

☐ EDIBLE UNDERPANTS = "Excruciatingly embarrassing for you, hilarious for everyone else." **1 POINT**

☐ AN AMUSING MUG = "I think I know your sense of humor." **2 POINTS**

☐ ONE OF THOSE SILLY BOOKS ABOUT TESTING YOUR COWORKERS, UGH = "We can pass this around the office and have a giggle." **3 POINTS**

☐ A PERSONALIZED PLAYLIST = "I wouldn't make this kind of effort for everyone." **4 POINTS**

☐ A BOOK BY YOUR FAVORITE WRITER = "I know you'll like this and will actually read it." **5 POINTS**

Chapter Four

MONARCHS AND MARTYRS

In this final chapter, it's time to take a seat on the other side of the desk and look at things from the other perspective. More often than not, bosses have a boss or two of their own—or even an entire boardroom of execs, shareholders, VPs, and senior VPs to answer to. It's rarely an easy gig. Overseeing all the junior drones—while simultaneously suffering the whims of the senior Big Cheeses—is like voluntarily placing one's head into an industrial vice. It is not uncommon for people in such a position to feel the cerebral squeeze of middle management on a daily (or even hourly) basis.

Bosses are not just people paid a bit extra to tell you what to do—they're also linchpins, negotiators, counselors, mediators, hagglers, facilitators, producers, brokers, and peacemakers.

And on top of all this, many of them have to handle their own dry cleaning. So, like it or loathe it, it's time to show them a little bit of love.

CHAPTER QUOTIENT: M*F POINTS

The scores in this chapter should indicate higher, moderate, or lower levels of MF or the "Martyrdom Factor."

SCORING NOTE: the higher scores in this section will probably result from situations in which your boss succeeds in protecting your own interests and/or professional position—to the best of his/her ability—while also towing the corporate line that has been flung down for you all to latch on to.

1 TRANSLATING THE TRASH

Whether you work in retail, agriculture, law, for a nonprofit, public service, or the media (to name but a few vocations), somewhere in the background there'll be a chain of command silently coiling itself around you and your coworkers. To do your job, you report into your team leader or line manager—and it's that person's job to pass down and interpret the corporate messages and directives cascading down from On High.

The way in which your boss handles this position is crucial to your general wellbeing at work. He or she needs to work out whether to drip-feed the information, force-feed it to you all at once, or dish it up on a need-to-know basis—while also making it palatable and easy to digest. Too much information about the state of the company's finances might choke you, while too little will leave you feeling starved and unworthy.

How well does your manager communicate and interpret messages and directives from the senior levels of management?

☐ Our team leader is often visibly agitated or annoyed when coming out of meetings with the senior execs—but we never find out why. (**NIL POINTS**)

☐ The boss passes the information only to senior members of the team, leaving everyone else to speculate and gossip about what might be going on. (**I POINT**)

☐ Corporate emails to our manager just get forwarded directly to the team, with no interpretation or explanation as to how the new directives affect us. (**2 POINTS**)

☐ He/she passes on and explains information to us regularly, but does it all by email. (**3 POINTS**)

☐ My manager talks to us individually or in small groups—to explain the relevance of what's happening—before a corporate announcement is officially made.
(**4 POINTS**)

☐ We have regular catch-ups with our boss, in which he/she invites us to ask questions about recent company announcements or directives. (**5 POINTS**)

2 PERSONABLE POSTURES

We've looked at a lot of boss-based body language already, but we haven't yet delved into the subtler levels of physical communication in the workplace. If you've worked with your current supervisors for a while, you may have become blind to the visual signals they are giving off when they're interacting with you.

Just for a few days, see if you can pay a bit more attention to any deliberate postures or delicate gestures. He or she may have done a course on face-to-face management, in which case it would be churlish to ignore the fruits of their labors.

SCORING NOTE: you may award MF points in each of the three sections that follow.

When your Alpha Dog comes to talk to you or bring you into a meeting, does he/she …

PART ONE: THE APPROACH

☐ hover in the corridor or doorway, as if only staying for a few moments? **NIL POINTS**

☐ come right over to your desk? **1 POINT**

☐ sit near you, on your level, but not facing you?
2 POINTS

☐ sit down and face you directly, on the same level as you?
3 POINTS

PART TWO: THE VERBAL ENGAGEMENT

☐ stand over you, looking and talking down at you?
NIL POINTS

☐ place hands on hips, while talking, to increase managerial wingspan? **1 POINT**

☐ appear calm and pleasant, with an unforced smile?
2 POINTS

☐ make eye contact when speaking to you?
3 POINTS

PART THREE: THE GROUP INTERACTION

☐ cross arms, fidget, wag or drum his/her fingers,
impatiently? **NIL POINTS**

☐ talk generally, rather than addressing individuals directly?
1 POINT

☐ smile, hands visible, with a generally open body posture?
2 POINTS

☐ introduce you to any unfamiliar or senior people in the
meeting? **3 POINTS**

TOTAL MF POINTS: _____

3 MIDNIGHT COWBOYS

In the language of 17th-century England, the word elucubrate meant to work long and intensively by lamplight. This suggests that many white-collar quill-pushers of the time worked pretty long hours. We still talk of "burning the midnight oil" today, harking back to a time (before the advent of electric lighting) when people used oil-fuelled lamps to toil away at their tasks well into the night.

Staying late in the office means different things to different people. If you're paid to do overtime, it can be a good thing—but if there's no remuneration for your extra-curricular activities, you could end up both physically and financially short-changed. Generally speaking, it's up to your leaders to set the pace. If they don't expect or encourage work outside of contractual hours, they should say so. And if they have to do it themselves, but don't like it, they shouldn't make you pay for it through the corporate currency of blame and guilt.

What is your leader's general attitude to working late?

☐ GLARER: if my boss is still working when I leave
the office on time, he/she always gives me a weird look.

NIL POINTS

☐ LIFER: the main reason my manager works late is
because he/she has absolutely no life outside the office.

I POINT

☐ EAGER BEAVER: my supervisor seems happy to work
late. He's/she's passionate about the job and likes to keep on
top of it. **2 POINTS**

☐ LONE WOLF: I suspect that my boss works late so
that we don't have to. He/she knows how badly we're paid.

3 POINTS

☐ NIGHTLY OWL: my boss makes it clear that he/she is
setting a very bad example by always staying late in the office.

4 POINTS

☐ TRIBAL CHIEF: my manager spends a lot of the day in
meetings or supporting the work of the team and has to
attend to his/her inbox after hours. **5 POINTS**

4 THE BLAME GAME

Nobody's perfect. You can be top of your game on Tuesday, then drop the ball on Wednesday. It happens. The trick is to try and get some consistency and avoid racking up too many blunders in a row, so that you don't end up on the radar as someone that needs babysitting.

There's a broad spectrum of patience among managers. Some are very tolerant of mistakes, always offering a second chance and some assistance where it's needed. Others may see errors as irreparable chinks in your armor, never trusting you with those tasks again.

In an ideal world, the office shouldn't be a place where people live in fear of failure. Employees should be able to fess up to their faults without heads rolling. But do we work in a ideal world?

How does your boss handle it when you make a mistake?

☐ BALL-BUSTING: we all live in fear of failing or missing our targets. I've witnessed colleagues being publicly flogged and hung out to dry. **NIL POINTS**

☐ COWERING: when it comes to errors, my boss is very non-confrontational. He/she always escalates staff discipline to a higher level. **I POINT**

☐ CONDESCENDING: even if it's a rare or trivial mistake, we have to have a sit-down meeting about "how we can prevent this from happening again … " **2 POINTS**

☐ SCAFFOLDING: he/she always offers support or training, as and when necessary, to help us minimize the impact of our mistakes. **4 POINTS**

☐ COLLABORATING: my boss tends to take equal responsibility for mistakes, support us, and give us the confidence to put things right again. **5 POINTS**

5 WORKPLACE BULLIES

On the plains of the Serengeti, the top predators pick off
and devour the weaker animals to reduce the population
and maintain the delicate balance of this wonderful
ecosystem. Bitching about someone behind his/her back, or
resenting a colleague because he or she has a nicer cubicle,
isn't quite so easy to justify.

In the brutal cut-throat environment of the workplace,
bullying can take many forms—there's deliberate exclusion
or avoidance, personal or work-related prejudice,
belittlement over the phone, intimidation by email, subtle
condescension, and/or face-to-face browbeating. It's a
common problem, so it's good to have a Head Honcho
who is prepared to engage with the creeping tendrils of
bullying—and hoist them out by their roots.

How well does your line manager deal with (and defuse) the presence of work-related bullying?

☐ More often than not, my manager is the perpetrator.
MINUS 1 POINT

☐ The last time I reported a problem with a coworker, my boss told me to "man up and grow a pair." **NIL POINTS**

☐ If a case of bullying is highlighted, my supervisor gets HR to deal with it. **1 POINT**

☐ My boss is usually oblivious to what's going on, but will engage with it one-to-one once the problem has been reported. **3 POINTS**

☐ My boss is incredibly approachable and understanding, so I know I'd be supported in response to bullying.
4 POINTS

☐ My manager seems to have a sixth sense for these things, stamping out a bad situation before it has even had a chance to develop. **5 POINTS**

6 BIGGING YOU UP

Your leader can't always be a cheerleader. He or she can't spend all day singing your praises, whooping your every move, dishing out high-fives and shoulder massages every time you do something AWW-SUMM!!—such as hit your sales target or unleash a stunningly worded email to the senior execs.

That said, it's nice to be appreciated once in a while, and a good boss will know how to keep your spirits up with a regular sprinkling of thanks and praise. Ideally, you should also feel as if your line manager is gunning for you in terms of promotion and/or professional development opportunities—so long as you're not the sort of slacker who doesn't deserve the hype!

How well do your taskmasters recognize and celebrate your merits?

☐ It makes no difference if I put in the maximum or minimum effort—my boss doesn't notice either way.
NIL POINTS

☐ I feel that my boss is a bit too liberal with his/her praise. Some of my colleagues need a kick up the ass, not a pat on the back. **1 POINT**

☐ My boss blows hot and cold. One day I'm overpraised for the simplest things—the next, slapped down for some trivial error or oversight. **1 POINT**

☐ If our team has performed well, we always get a shout out at the company-wide meetings. **3 POINTS**

☐ My boss is a master of the well-timed compliment. He/she always knows when I'm struggling and need a bit of a confidence boost. **4 POINTS**

☐ My supervisor always has one eye on my future, talking me up and encouraging me to do some extra training or go for promotion. **5 POINTS**

7 A SIMPLE TRANSACTION

When you think about it, going to work involves a very simple equation: attendance + commitment + effort = regular pay, perks, pension, and (if you're lucky) bonuses. If your employers didn't pay you, you'd stop turning up; and if you stopped turning up, they wouldn't pay you.

But the thorny issue of fair pay doesn't end there. What if your pay never increased, or you were asked to take a temporary pay cut to aid the survival of the business? What if you found out that another colleague, at the same level as you, was being paid more? What if a rumor was being circulated, suggesting that your boss is about to receive a six-figure bonus? If any of those circumstances arose, would your boss be able to solve such a complex equation?

Are salary talks a dying art in your office?

☐ BOO!: my boss always seems to get a raise, even when raises have been frozen for the rest of the department.

NIL POINTS

☐ NO CAN DO: company bonuses are strictly discretionary, and pay raises are never openly discussed.

1 POINT

☐ "GOOD FOR YOU!": my manager is happy to talk about my salary, and registers the fact that I'm looking to slither up the career ladder and pay scale. **2 POINTS**

☐ NOT TABOO: our senior execs are always open, honest, and frank about the likelihood of bonuses and pay rises.

3 POINTS

☐ GOLDEN THANK YOU: if it's been a profitable year, my manager puts us all forward for merit-related bonuses.

4 POINTS

☐ WHA-HOO!: my boss once took a cut in pay—and/or forfeited his bonus—so that there'd be enough in the pot for the rest of us to get a raise. **5 POINTS**

8 THE "R" WORD

There's a scourge on the face of the corporate world, and it has a name: redundancy. In times of financial drought, shareholders get the shakes, clients go hungry, and company accountants suddenly morph into hooded executioners—with narrow profit margins as their sharpened blades. And if you're not lucky, your head may be one of the dispensable noggins thrust to the block.

Some people fear the R-word, some have become resigned to it (literally), others go with the flow and see it as an opportunity—and then there are those who have been waiting years for the great-big-fat pay-off they'll get when they're finally deemed surplus to requirements. Whatever the circumstances, it can be a pretty ugly, emotional, and gut-churning process to stomach, and if you don't have the support of your union, colleagues, and/or superiors … it could get a whole lot worse.

In the midst of a redundancy situation, how well does your boss stand up for you and your department?

☐ ONE IN, ONE OUT: as my manager once said to me, "Oh well … last in, first out, eh?" **NIL POINTS**

☐ ONE FOR THE ROAD: if the going gets tough, my boss'll take the cash and get going. **NIL POINTS**

☐ LOOKING AFTER NUMBER ONE: my manager's always keen to protect the jobs of those who work hard and make his/her life easier. **1 POINT**

☐ ONE-OFF FAVOR: he/she gave us a list of people we should contact for help and advice. **2 POINTS**

☐ ONE OF US: our line manager was a real support during the consultation process, suggesting questions to ask and reminding us of our rights. **3 POINTS**

☐ ONE AGAINST MANY: my supervisor has had lengthy meetings with HR and the senior execs, to try and get the best possible deal for those affected by redundancy.
4 POINTS

☐ TAKING ONE FOR THE TEAM: my boss would probably take an R-bullet and sacrifice him/herself, so that others would not have to lose their jobs. **5 POINTS**

THE EXECUTIVE LEVELS: THE SCORING

CHAPTER ONE

TESTING FOR TBD, or "True Boss DNA"

5—18 TBD POINTS:

This is the kind of workaholic who's somehow ended up in charge, but who lacks the training, interpersonal skills, and natural inclination to handle the job effectively. He or she lives for their own work, but finds the idea of overseeing the labors of other people inconvenient and, frankly, a bit of a drag.

19—32 TBD POINTS:

Someone with this level of TBD is possibly a bit too hung up on the idea of being the boss. He or she is very conscious of status, but doesn't always think too deeply about what it means to lead the troops. Such people are committed to the job, in their own way, but some of the key leadership and interpersonal skills may be lacking.

33—43 TBD POINTS:

These scores point to a person who is either a natural leader or has adapted well to the demands of management. This is a professional but fair-minded person who doesn't feel the need to exert too much power over (or heap too much pressure onto) junior staff members.

CHAPTER TWO

GUNNING FOR GURU GRADES (GGs)

1—15 GGs:

Being managed by this person can be an uncomfortable and sometimes embarrassing experience. There's very little active leadership on show, and whenever he/she does acknowledge you (and your work) the intervention is neither helpful nor warranted. There's a lack of trust and understanding between the Head Honcho and the general staff, morale in the team is low, and people are always on the lookout for other jobs.

16—28 GGs:

These bosses can be very neurotic—intense, insecure, and overbearing. They are highly opinionated, obsessed with their work and expect you—as an employee—to be cast from the exact same mold as themselves. Their managerial style is corporate and thorough, but perhaps a bit too hands-on and heavy-handed at times. Working for this person, you'll either end up incredibly overworked or a little bit bored.

29—39 GGs:

Yeah, man, this is what you're looking for—a boss you can look up to and respect, without feeling like you have to be his or her best buddy. You'll feel supported (but not smothered), championed (but not choked), and you might even look forward to sharing your working day with this person. Such a leader is capable of looking out for pretty much everyone in the team, from people with ambition to those who prefer to fade into the background.

CHAPTER THREE

SEARCHING FOR HQ, the "Human Quotient"

4—23 HQ POINTS:

This person really struggles to have any meaningful or proactive contact with other human beings in the office environment (or anywhere else for that matter). Some will fail to interact with you when it's necessary to do so, some are socially awkward by nature, while others may offer their attentions in a wholly unwelcome or inappropriate way.

24—37 HQ POINTS:

If your boss falls into this category, don't panic. You're working under a safe pair of hands, who does his/her job carefully, meticulously, and by the numbers … but don't expect too many backslaps and wisecracks. This one's a cold fish with a stiff upper lip, who may work you hard and bust your balls at times—but you'll never be unduly harassed or bullied on his/her watch.

38—54 HQ POINTS:

Bosses like these don't come around too often, so try and bask in the glow of this caring, considerate, approachable supervisor while you can. Even if you're currently earning peanuts, you might want to stay under the spotlight of this bright-and-bold visionary for a little while longer—before chasing the bigger bucks elsewhere—because he'll/she'll value you, nurture you, and develop your career in ways that money can't buy.

CHAPTER FOUR

MEASURING THE MARTYRDOM FACTOR (MF)

MINUS 1—18 MF POINTS:

"Bad communicator" doesn't even begin to describe this type of boss. Such managers rely on their professional status to provide a modicum of self-esteem, they probably suffer from a poor family or social life—and may even resent you for having a more prosperous one. They do very little to cushion you from the corporate bombshells dropped from the upper levels of management, and they have no time for human error. If you're suffering from any work-based anxiety, bullying, or harassment, it's likely that this Head Honcho is at least partly to blame.

19—31 MF POINTS:

Being one of the crew under this captain is like being the middle child of nine siblings. You generally feel provided for, but you're just begging for a little more lovin'! (Hey, just a soupçon of recognition and appreciation would be a start). This person will keep your job ticking over, providing all of the boss-like basics, but he'll/she'll never lay down their professional reputation in exchange for your personal wellbeing.

32—44 MF POINTS:

Climb onto this bus, Comrades, because the driver goes the extra mile! You'll never lack motivation under this master, because you'll always feel involved in his/her thought processes, and confident that your role, opinions, and contributions are important. You won't be expected to do more than what's in your job description—but if you're keen to reach up to the next level, you'll be given the right kind of platform. This person creates a protective, family-like atmosphere, too, wading into the depths to keep you all afloat when the waters of work start to run fast and deep.

Overall Analysis

Now's the time to total up your boss's scores and see which rank he/she has achieved in the overall Hierarchy of Head Honchos …

9—74 POINTS: THE PETTY OFFICER

If your leader has fallen into this range, you're probably feeling a bit depressed right now. But don't despair. You probably won't be reporting to such a boss for long, because this kind of Big Kahuna finds it hard to hold on to the people around them, especially the ones with talent and good prospects. You'll be drawn to pastures new before too long, leaving this person to wallow in the inadequate managerial quagmire of his/her own making. His/her only saving grace is the fact that he/she probably didn't want to be a boss in the first place.

75—129 POINTS: THE COMPETENT COLONEL

On a purely professional level, you'll find it hard to criticize the manager who falls into this category. Technically, he/she's doing nothing wrong … It's just that you'd like something more, some extra little *je ne sais quoi* to make your working day a little bit more bearable. The good thing about these bosses is that they get the job done. They keep the department afloat and make sure your job is relatively secure, your prospects more or less on track. The trouble is, they're just a wee bit too aware of their position at the top of the tree, often subjecting you to their intensive ways of working. But when all's said and done, they're not paid to be your best buddies … So suck it up, slackers!!

130 POINTS AND ABOVE: THE MAJOR GENERAL

Congratulations—you've won the Leadership Lottery! If your supervisor has made it into this upper range, you really won't have much to complain about. Heck, you might even have a little spring in your step when you next stroll to the office. With this Great Guru in charge, you'll learn while you earn and—if you put your hands to the pump—set up the foundations for a pretty decent career. The exemplary qualities of a natural or experienced manager tend to rub off on the people around him/her, which means everyone achieves and has a better chance of going places … So strap yourselves in, Troops, and serve in the company of the Major General!

ACKNOWLEDGMENTS

I wrote this book in the fourth year of self-employment as an author and editorial manager. So I'm one of those people who has both "no boss" and "many bosses" (my clients and publishers) at the same time. To come up with these tests and observations, I've drawn on seventeen years of working in and out of offices and in publishing houses all over London, so I'd really like to thank all of the wonderfully talented and creative people I've had the pleasure of working with in this incredible city. Plying one's trade in a place like London is akin to playing an arcade game calibrated to its fastest and most difficult setting—all of the flipping time—so while I've poked a bit of fun at the managers I've worked both with and for over the years, I'd also like to congratulate them (well, most of them!) for at least attempting the impossible feat of keeping a hamster wheel turning while making sure all the other rodents are entertained, too. I'd also like to thank the lovely Caitlin Doyle, at HarperCollins, for keeping me busy.